Emma Dilemma

Big Sister Poems

BY Kristine O'Connell George

ILLUSTRATED BY Nancy Carpenter

CLARION BOOKS

HOUGHTON MIFFLIN HARCOURT

BOSTON • NEW YORK

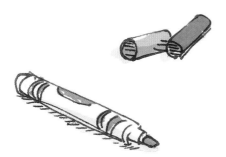

Clarion Books

215 Park Avenue South, New York, New York 10003

Text copyright © 2011 by Kristine O'Connell George

Illustrations copyright © 2011 by Nancy Carpenter

The text was set in 14-point Stone Informal.
The illustrations were executed in pen and ink and digital media.

Clarion Books is an imprint of Houghton Mifflin Harcourt Publishing Company.

www.hmhbooks.com

Library of Congress Cataloging-in-Publication Data

George, Kristine O'Connell.
Emma dilemma : big sister poems / by Kristine O'Connell George ; illustrated by Nancy Carpenter.
p. cm.
ISBN 978-0-618-42842-7
1. Sisters—Juvenile poetry.   2. Children's poetry, American.   I. Title.

PS3557.E488 B54 2009

811'.54—dc22

2008050647

Manufactured in China

LEO   10   9   8   7   6   5   4   3   2

4500274658

For Lynne Whaley,
my almost sister
—K.O.G.

For Maeve, the best big sister any
little brother (or sister) could ask for
—N.C.

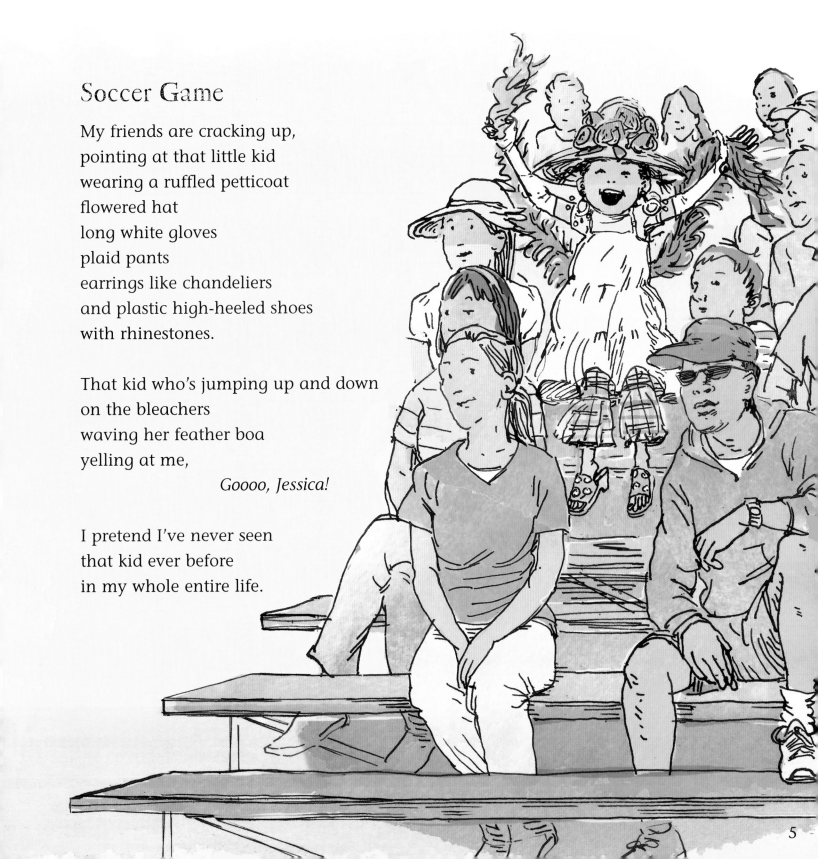

Soccer Game

My friends are cracking up,
pointing at that little kid
wearing a ruffled petticoat
flowered hat
long white gloves
plaid pants
earrings like chandeliers
and plastic high-heeled shoes
with rhinestones.

That kid who's jumping up and down
on the bleachers
waving her feather boa
yelling at me,
            Goooo, Jessica!

I pretend I've never seen
that kid ever before
in my whole entire life.

Stuff Grownups Say

I wish grownups would quit saying
we LOOK like sisters . . .
because I told Emma
we got her at the hardware store.

I wish grownups would quit saying
    I'll bet you're
    a very good big sister.

Know what? They never ask Emma
if she is a very good *little* sister.

    Not once.
    Not ever.

Role Model

Emma copies
everything I do,
and sometimes
I don't do
something
I might do
or really
want to do
because
I know
she is
always
watching
every single thing I do.

Emma's Hand

Emma's hand is
    just the right size
    to fit
    inside mine.

Emma's hand is
    warm
    soft
    friendly

    sticky.

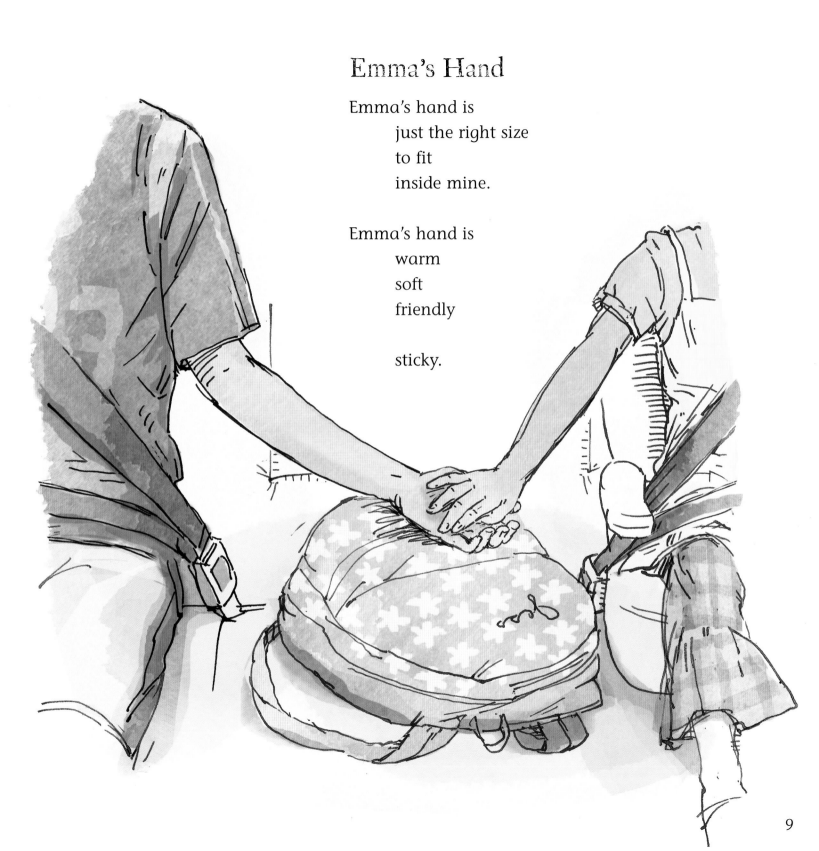

Emma Dilemma

Sometimes Dad
calls my little sister
Emma Dilemma.

Dad says
a dilemma is
an interesting problem.

I know Dad's joking,
but sometimes
Emma *is* my dilemma.

Translator

I am often the only one
who understands
Emma Language:

Nostrils are *nozzles*.
My calculator is a *count-a-lator*.
Loodle loos are peaches,
which Emma eats for breakfast
with her *squabbled eggs*.

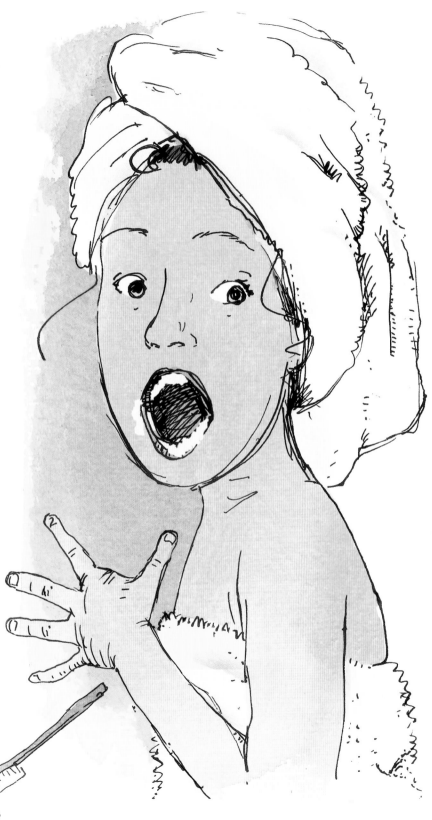

Dracula

Emma leaps out at me.
    Cape.
    Fangs.
    Fake blood.

    Scared you!
    Scared you!

Did not!
Did not!

    Did too!

Did not!
I *like* to start the day
with a scream.

Late for School

I am late for school,
first day of fourth grade,
can't find one shoe—
when a sports-shoe car
loaded with rock people
powered by a little sister
         speeds by . . .

My sneaker!

I stop the race,
dump the rocks,
yell at Emma,
put on my shoes,
and run for the bus
         just as Emma
         starts to cry.

Fun with Yarn

After school I open the door to my room,
find yards and yards of yarn looped everywhere
from lamp to dresser to bed.

Emma stands behind me, giggling.
Big spidey web, Jess!

That little spider had better
unweave her web
before I

          squash her.

Bed Partner

Late at night—
    the sound of duck slippers
    pounding down the hall.
    Emma crawling into bed with me
    because she thought there were
    huge monsters in her room.

Early morning—
   waking up icy cold
   because a certain little monster
   is hogging all the covers.

Collector

One of the reasons
Emma loves me
is that I am the only one
who can remember
the names of all her
rocks.

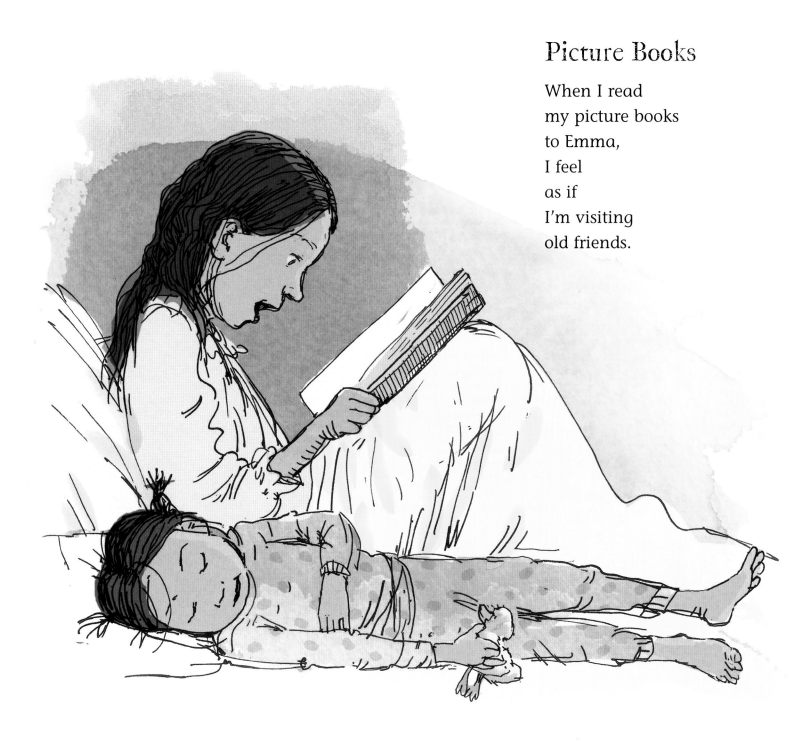

Picture Books

When I read
my picture books
to Emma,
I feel
as if
I'm visiting
old friends.

Funny

I told a joke at school
and no one laughed.
I told the joke at dinner
and Emma laughed so hard,
her milk came out her nose.

Mom and Dad said I can't
tell that joke
at dinner
ever again.

Not Funny

Emma's knock-knock jokes
go like this:

Emma: *Knock! Knock!*
Me: Who's there?
Emma: *Banana.*
Me: Banana who?
Emma: *. . . I forgot!*

Then Emma rolls on the floor,
    can't stop laughing at her joke.

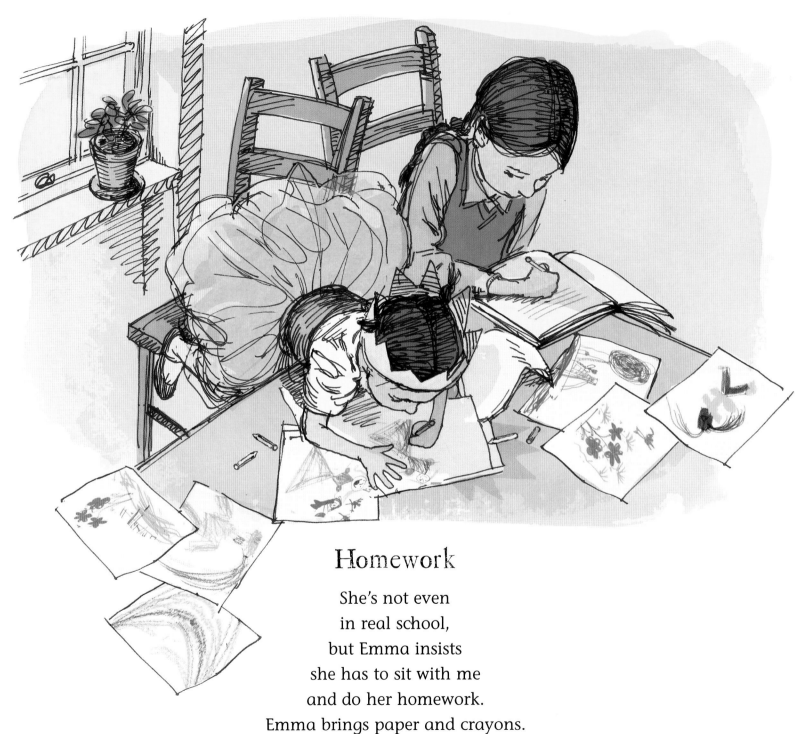

Homework

She's not even
in real school,
but Emma insists
she has to sit with me
and do her homework.
Emma brings paper and crayons.
I move over, give her plenty of elbow room,
because the pictures inside Emma's head are bigger than the kitchen table.

Family Tree

My homework is a family tree.
I draw
      branches for my grandparents
      branches for Mom and Dad
      a branch for Uncle Dick
      a branch for me
and a teeny twig for Emma.

Snooping

One good thing about a little sister
is that if I give her a boost
she can reach
that mysterious box
hidden
on the top shelf.

One bad thing about a little sister
is that she can't keep secrets.
When my secrets
are inside Emma,
they leak out slowly,
like air out of a balloon,
or fast —
in one enormous
Tattletale Explosion.

Fine Dining

When Mom and Dad
aren't looking,
I show Emma
the *right* way

to blow

the paper
off the straw.

Sharing

Mom says Emma and I
get to share
the piece of cherry pie
she can't finish.

I get to cut it in half—
Emma gets to choose first.

I am so very careful,
making sure
that both halves
are very, very equal.

Cheating

Emma cheats
at board games
and card games
and *still* loses.

She cries so hard
that Mom says,
> *Why can't you let*
> *your little sister win*
> *just once?*

So I teach Emma
52-Card Pick-Up.
The floor is covered
in a blizzard of cards.
So why is Mom mad?
Why do *I* have to pick up
every single card?

Emma's Birthday

Emma used to say, *I'm twee!*
Today she's four, and she thinks
she's as old as me.

Emma asks me to help her
think of a name for the new duck
I gave her for her birthday.

I suggest a truly excellent name:
Janey Green-Bill Sara Turnpike Eater-of-Snails Webbed-Feet Feather Fluff Duck.

Emma names her new duck

    Quack.

Trespass

Someone
has been "shopping"
in my room.

Someone
has been playing
dress-up with my clothes.

Someone
left the caps off
all my new markers.

Someone
drew a face
on my soccer ball.

Someone is hiding
and had better hope
I never find her.

Justice

Enough is enough.
I show Mom and Dad
my long list
of all the times
Emma has invaded
my room.

The shiny lock Dad puts
on my bedroom door
is like a sign,
a sign that says:
>This is Jessica's room.
>No trespassing!

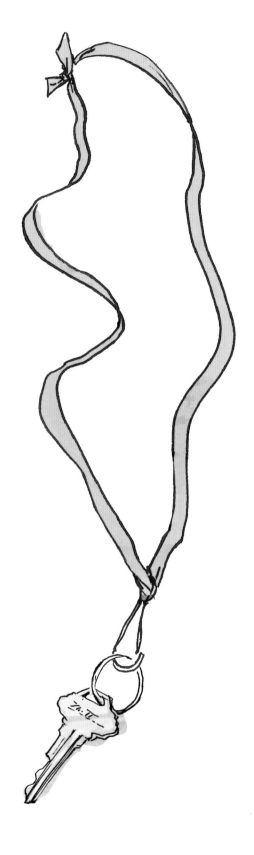

Telling Time

I show Emma
the big hand on the twelve,
the little hand on the six.
      See? Six o'clock.

Emma skips off singing:
      Dinner time!
      Sunset pink time!
      Silverware clink time!

Accident

Emma races to tell me:

> I was dancing.
> The tree
> in the pot
> in the living room
> spilled its dirt
> all over the floor.
>
> It fainted!

I feel good and kind of bad
when I say:

> Just wait, Emma.
> Just wait until
> Mom finds out.

Comfort

I got a bad grade
on my spelling test.

Emma, who doesn't even know
what grades are,
sees how sad I am,
guesses how awful I feel.

Emma tells me
she's full of sorry,
cuddles up next to me,
pats my arm,
says I can hold Quack

for

one

whole

hour.

Field Trip

I have three dollars
to buy a souvenir
on our class field trip
to the natural history museum.

I buy a purple
sparkly rock
for Emma.

Freedom

My best friend, Sasha, comes over,
and Mom promises—
cross her heart—
that she'll keep Emma
        out of our way.

I have my friend all to myself—
no Emma
stuck to me
like a burr
stuck to my sock.

Oak

Sasha and I climb
to the top of the oak,
sit in my treehouse,
tell secrets.

I think I hear
Emma down below,
but I don't look down.

Sasha whispers:
> Emma's got a chair.
> I think she's going to try
> to climb our tree.

But I don't look down
        until
                I hear
                        Emma fall.

39

Below

Emma, so small
below me
on the ground.
Not moving.
Just crying.

I'm cold all over,
shaking as I climb
down out of the tree,
down to Emma.

I hold Emma's hand
as Sasha runs
to get Mom.

Mom kneels down,
speaks softly to Emma,
brushes back her bangs.

Mom's voice is tight,
full of tears,
when she asks,
        What happened, Jessica?

Mom's voice is like ice
when she says,
        I think Emma's arm is broken.

I can't talk.
I can't say one single word.

Hospital

Mom takes Emma
to the hospital.
I rescue Quack
from under the tree.

I'm supposed to wait
at Sasha's house.
I sit on Sasha's metal glider,
pushing off again and again,
the glider scraping
a sound for my thoughts:

My fault.
My fault.

Return

The sun is almost down
when Dad scoops me up
and walks me home.

Emma is asleep in Mom's arms.
Her eyelashes make
soft shadows on her cheeks.
Her pink cast
looks heavy and hard.

I gently tuck Quack
under her good arm.
Mom smiles.
You're such a good big sister.

I'm not.

43

Confession

Emma is still asleep.
It's just the three of us at dinner.
Suddenly I'm crying.
Suddenly I'm saying:
It's all my fault.
I should have stopped Emma.
I should have let her
play with us.

Mom stares at me,
pulls me into her lap.

> *No. Not your fault, Jessica.*
> *Emma was too quick for me.*
> *It was an accident.*

Not my fault?
Not my fault?
But you were so angry, Mom.

> *Oh, Jess. I wasn't angry. I was scared.*

Mom and Dad take turns
holding me tight.
I melt into their arms,
melt into those good words—
> An accident.
> Not my fault.
> Not my fault.

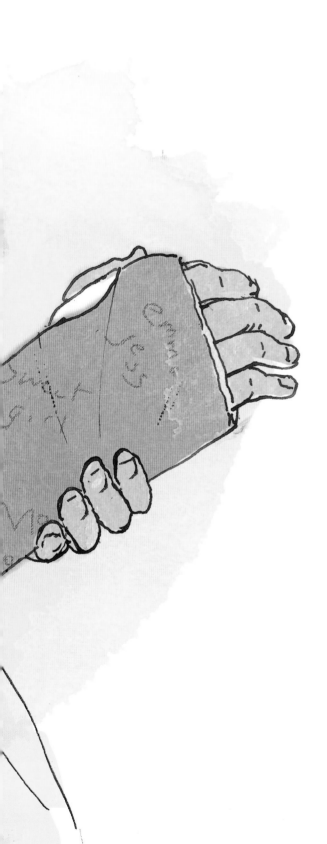

Cast

Emma wants me to
be the first one
to sign her cast.
I print

I love you Emma

with the only marker I have left
that Emma hasn't ruined.
I don't say one word
about her leaving the caps off.

I think of something else,
and I carefully write

You
   are
     my
Emma Dilemma.